THE HISTORY DETECTIVE INVESTIGATES

D1635766

Tudor Home

Alan Childs

HODDER
Wayland

an imprint of Hodder Children's Books

728

N

The History Detective series
Tudor Home
Tudor Medicine
Tudor Theatre
Tudor War
Victorian Crime
Victorian Factory
Victorian School
Victorian Transport

For more information on this series and other Hodder Wayland titles, go to www.hodderwayland.co.uk

First published in Great Britain in 2002 by Hodder Wayland, an imprint of Hodder Children's Books
Reprinted in 2005
© Copyright 2002 Hodder Wayland

Hodder Children's Books
A division of Hodder Headline Limited
338 Euston Road, London NW1 3BH

Editor: Kay Barnham
Designer: Simon Borrough
Cartoon artwork: Richard Hook
Picture research: Shelley Noronha – Glass Onion Pictures

British Library Cataloguing in Publication Data

Childs, Alan, 1942-
The history detective investigates a Tudor house
        1. Dwellings - England - History - 16th century -
        Juvenile literature
        2. England - Social conditions - 16th century -
        Juvenile literature
        I. Title II. A Tudor house
        728' .0942'09031

ISBN 0 7502 3750 3

Printed in China

Picture acknowledgements:
The publishers would like to thank the following for permission to reproduce their pictures: Alan Childs 7 (right), 10 (right); GGS Photographics 19 (left); Hulton Getty Picture Library 19; Ingatestone Hall cover, 26, 27 (top & bottom); The Bridgeman Art Library 4, 5 (top) (Mark Fiennes), cover, 13 (right), 14, 16 (bottom) (Christie's Images), 17, 18, 23; The Fotomas Index Picture Library 25; Mary Evans Picture Library 20 (bottom), 24, 29; Museum of London 13 (left), 16 (top), 19 (bottom); National Trust Photographic Library: 1, 28 (Andrew Butler), 22 (bottom) (Andrea Jones), 21 (Nadia MacKenzie), 4 (bottom) (John Miller), cover, 6, 11 (left) (Geoff Morgan), cover, 9 (top & bottom) (Erik Pelham), 22 (top) (Mike Williams), cover (Rupert Truman); Royal Collection 15 (bottom); Weald and Downland Museum 7 (left), 8, 12; Wayland Picture Library cover, 10 (right), 15 (top), 20 (top).

Contents

What were Tudor homes like?

*I*magine a home where the toilet was a plank over a pit and where glass windows were so valuable they were left in a will. If you owned a carpet, you did not walk on it – you displayed it on a table, or the wall!

The Tudor period lasted from 1485 to 1603. When the first Tudor monarch came to the throne, timber was usually used to build houses. However, by the time Elizabeth I was crowned in 1558, timber had become rarer and more expensive, because so many trees had been cut down and not replanted in the past. Luckily, bricks were now cheap enough for many people to use instead.

The history detective, Sherlock Bones, will help you to find clues and collect evidence about Tudor homes – how they were built and what it was like to live in them. Wherever you see one of Sherlock's paw-prints, you will find a mystery to solve. The answers can be found on pages 30 and 31.

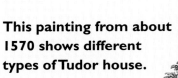

This painting from about 1570 shows different types of Tudor house.

The smallest Tudor houses have not survived. These were tiny cottages built of wood and clay, their earth floors hardened with bull's blood. Only the bigger houses and grand mansions still stand today. Burghley House in Lincolnshire is one of the finest. It was built between 1565 and 1587 by William Cecil, the most important man in Elizabeth I's government.

DETECTIVE WORK

Try to find Tudor houses in your area. Your nearest large library may be able to help. Remember, they may not look like Tudor buildings now. Beams may have been covered over and windows changed. But there are clues for the careful history detective.

Burghley House is built from local limestone.

A Tudor cottage.

An Italian visitor described how the English built their homes:

First they construct a frame of wood joined together with wooden pegs and then between one layer of wood and another they put bricks. The houses have many windows in which they put glass that's almost as clear as crystal. Inside, the houses are… decorated with wood carving… On the floors they put straw… For wall coverings they use many tapestries woven with leaves, flowers and beautiful… designs.

Alessandro Magno, 1562

✿ Why do you think that the smallest Tudor houses have not survived?

How were Tudor homes built?

Tudor streets were very dark places, because of the way timbered houses were built. Each storey jutted out a little further than the one below – sometimes by more than a metre. The overhangs were called jetties. Sometimes, the houses were so close together at the top, it was said you could shake hands with your neighbour across the street!

DETECTIVE WORK

Find examples of timbered houses or farm buildings in books and on the Internet – there may even be some examples near your school. Make drawings or take photos of the beam patterns. Can you find examples of jetties? How far do they overhang?

Little Moreton Hall (left) is in Congleton, Cheshire. Building started in the 1440s, and was finally completed in 1580.

✿ Why do you think Tudor houses were built with jetties?

Little Moreton Hall has fantastic patterns made from wooden beams. Blackening the beams with paint or tar was a later fashion. In Tudor times, the beams would be left as natural 'silvery' wood, or covered with plaster.

One Tudor man came home to find that his house had been moved by a rich neighbour, who wanted to steal his land. His son tells the story:

'My father had a garden there, and a house… this house they loosed from the ground, and bare [carried] upon rollers into my father's garden 22 feet [over six metres]… No warning was given him.'

John Stowe, *A Survey of London* (1598)

The Tudors used newly cut wood – usually oak, elm or ash – to build a timbered house, because this was easier to saw. Tree trunks were laid across a saw-pit, and cut with an enormous two-man saw. One sawyer stood in the pit and the other on the edge of it. A special tool called an 'adze' was then used to smooth the wood.

Carpenters often cut all the joints for a new house in their own yard, numbering them so that they could be put together on the site.

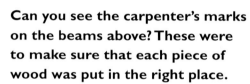

Can you see the carpenter's marks on the beams above? These were to make sure that each piece of wood was put in the right place.

In later houses, bricks were used to fill the gaps between beams.

In early Tudor houses, especially in the countryside, the spaces between the wooden frame were filled with small woven sticks called 'wattle'. These were covered with a 'daub' of mud, clay and cow-dung, mixed with straw or cow hair. It was a messy, smelly job! Later, flat pieces of wood called 'laths' were used across the gaps instead. Walls were then covered with plaster.

Did the Tudors invent chimneys?

DETECTIVE WORK

If it is possible to visit a large Tudor house, look carefully at the chimneys, perhaps using binoculars. See how the patterned bricks make up a design and sketch some of the interesting designs you find. Look out for chimneys which have been built on to the end of the building.

Chimneys had been around for centuries before Tudor times, but in the sixteenth century they were still very rare. Most early houses were made up of one big room or 'hall', with the same kind of smoke holes in the roof that had been used for hundreds of years. Fires were made in the middle of the 'hall' and smoke had to find its way out of the smoke hole, or through cracks and windows. Homes were smoky, with everything covered in soot and tar.

This early flint and straw-thatch cottage has the type of smoke hole that was used until Tudor times.

One Tudor writer said that old men living in his village noted great changes in the houses:

'One [change] is the multitude of chimneys lately erected, whereas in their young days there were not above two or three, if so many, in most uplandish towns of the realm…'

William Harrison, *A Description of England* (1577-87)

Cheap bricks made it possible for the Tudors to become the first people to use chimneys in most houses. At first, it was easier to add chimneys on to an end wall, but later the chimneys were built at the same time as the house. Inside, there would be large fireplaces called 'inglenooks'. These were like small rooms, where you could sit and warm yourself.

Chimneys changed people's lives. Smoky rooms became a thing of the past and homes could have rooms upstairs. The extra floor could be built because smoke no longer had to find its way out of the smoke hole. Families now also had parlours – private areas downstairs that were away from the large halls.

☙ Why do you think it was easier to build the first chimneys on to the ends of the houses?

This Tudor merchant's house in Tenby, Wales, has an end chimney.

Fireplaces made it easier to burn coal. This provided more heat than wood, so homes became warmer.

Could the Tudors afford glass windows?

It is difficult to think of windows not being made of glass. But glass was too expensive for many Tudors. The word window means 'wind eye' – an eye for the wind to blow through. In the days before glass, this is just what the wind did!

By Tudor times glass was becoming much more common. But, other window coverings were still used: wooden shutters which slid up and down in grooves; flattened cows' horn; oiled cloth; and parchment dipped in gum, honey and egg-white. Sometimes, windows were covered with reeds or even pieces of very thin stone. Unfortunately, when these windows were closed, the rooms were dark – and when they were open, the rooms were often cold.

Lattice windows could be very plain...

... or very ornamental.

❀ Do you think that the designs in the windows on the left are just for decoration? Or do they stand for something?

The Tudors could make whole sheets of glass, but the soft lead fittings that held the panes together could not be relied upon to secure large panes in strong winds. Instead, windows were made up of smaller panes of glass held together with strips of soft lead. These were called lattice windows.

DETECTIVE WORK

Visit a local church and look carefully at the windows. In most old churches, you will be able to see how small pieces of glass are held in place by metal strips. This is exactly how Tudor windows were made. Now compare these windows to the lattice windows in modern houses. How are they different?

As late as 1567, the owner of Alnwick Castle in Northumberland removed and stored his windows when he was not at home. Windows were still very valuable, and had to be protected. Tudor house-builders, such as Elizabeth of Shrewsbury, made the most of their windows. There were so many of them in her Tudor mansion that it was said: 'Hardwick Hall, more glass than wall'.

'Of old time, our country houses, instead of glass did use much lattice, and that made either of wicker or fine rifts of oak in checkerwise… But… our lattices are also grown into less use, because glass is come to be so plentiful.'

William Harrison, *A Description of England* (1577-87)

☙ The owner of Hardwick Hall put her initials all over the house. Can you spot any of them?

Hardwick Hall, built between 1591 and 1597, was a great Tudor mansion.

What were Tudor beds like?

Tudor houses often had no landings – one upstairs room led into another. The large expensive beds called 'testers', or four-posters, had curtains around them – partly to keep out draughts, but also to save blushes if someone walked through your bedroom!

'Tester' beds were high off the ground, with enough room underneath to store a bed on wheels – called a 'truckle' bed. It was pulled out at night for a servant or child to sleep on.

DETECTIVE WORK

Contact your nearest County Record Office, and ask whether they have any Tudor inventories (lists of people's possessions when they died) for your area. They may have a translation, but sometimes you will have to read real Tudor handwriting! The bedstead is usually listed along with all its 'furniture' – the linen and hangings.

To a Tudor the word 'bed' probably meant just the mattress. The wooden frame was called a 'bedstead'. The mattress might be stuffed with wool, feathers from plucked poultry, straw, chaff (the husks and grass left from corn), and even thistledown. Bed coverings and curtains were washed only three or four times a year.

A strange, but cheap, filling for pillows and mattresses was thistledown – the furry seeds of the thistle:

'The common thistle, wherof the greatest quantity of down is gathered for divers (various) purposes, as well by the poor to stop (stuff) pillows, cushions, and beds for want of feathers, as also bought of the rich upholsters to mix with the feathers and down they do sell, which deceit would be looked into...'

John Gerard, *Historie of Plants* (1597)

❉ Why was thistledown mixed with feathers to make a stuffing for pillows and cushions? There are clues in the text above.

A very rich Tudor would have slept in this bed.

A Tudor warming pan.

Beds for poor people were simple wooden frames with ropes criss-crossed to support the mattress. 'Box beds' were often built into a wall, like a cupboard, to save space. As real beds were valuable, the Tudors often included them in their wills. When he died in 1616, Shakespeare left his 'second-best bed' to his wife Anne.

Only the rich wore night clothes – others slept in their underclothes. When the nights were colder, Tudors heated their beds with hot coals in a warming pan.

How did the Tudors 'pluck a rose'?

Indoor toilets were built out from the side of the house, with a pit below.

❦ What do you think the 'close stool' on page 15 was used for? And who might have used it?

Tudors went to the toilet where it suited them: by the roadside, into rivers and even in their own fireplaces. They called it 'plucking a rose'. They were also quite happy to tip the contents of their chamber pots out of bedroom windows into the street below.

The Tudor word for a toilet was 'jakes', but it was also known as a 'privy', a 'house of office', a 'stool room', or a 'necessary house'. A toilet was usually a plank over a pit in the garden. Even an indoor toilet was just a tiny room with a plank over a pit lined with ashes.

When the toilet was full, it had to be emptied. The 'gong farmer', or 'jakes farmer', cleared it out, mixing the contents with the ashes. This was then used as fertilizer. Gong farmers were paid well, as it was not a very popular job!

'Hookers' were Tudor thieves who used long hooks to steal people's clothes. One hooker hooked a chamber pot by accident!

'...his face, his head, and his neck were all besmeared... so he stunk worse than a jakes-farmer...'

Robert Greene, *The Black Book's Messenger* (1592)

Hampton Court Palace (above) had a 14-seater toilet!

In 1596, Sir John Harrington invented the first flushing toilet. Queen Elizabeth ordered one for Richmond Palace, but it was not popular.

King Henry VIII had problems getting his servants to use the jakes at Hampton Court Palace. A law of 1547 stated: 'No person… shall make water… within the precincts of the Court'.

This strange object is called a 'close stool'.

DETECTIVE WORK

Find out more about the history of toilets. The books listed on page 31 will help.

How clean were the Tudors?

Only someone as important as a king or queen had a proper bathroom. Henry VIII's bathroom in his palace at Hampton Court was splendid – it had a wall-mounted bath, with hot and cold running water. Rich Tudors bathed in a wooden tub in front of their bedroom fire, while poor people made do with a quick dip in a pond or river. Washing was not something that Tudors did every day.

A sweet-smelling pomander.

Rich Tudors like the painter Isaac Oliver wore grand clothes, but bathed very little.

Some people carried 'pomanders' around with them. These were containers full of sweet herbs, or oranges stuffed with cloves, to disguise everyone else's body odours!

Those with baths could afford scented soap, perfumed with almond or musk oil. Herbs would also be spread on the water. Ordinary people made their own soap for washing their clothes, or even to use on themselves. This was a smelly household job. Water that had been trickled through burnt wood ash, was strained and then mixed with animal fat.

Many Tudors washed their clothes in a wash-house by a river. Clothes were beaten clean with 'battling stones', before being spread out over bushes or on the ground to dry.

Many Tudors had smelly breath because of their bad teeth. Their love of sweet foods did not help. Even Queen Elizabeth's teeth were black and rotten. Tudors used a kind of toothpaste, called tooth soap, made from honey, vinegar and white wine. They put this on with their fingers. It probably did not help their teeth very much.

Having teeth pulled was a painful business in Tudor times. There was very little to numb the pain.

DETECTIVE WORK

None of Queen Elizabeth I's many portraits show her bad teeth. Can you guess why this is?

This is a recipe for Tudor soap:

'The leaves of the bramble boiled in water, with honey, alum (a kind of salt) and a little white wine added thereto, make a most excellent lotion or washing water, and the same decoction fastneth (the boiled mixture strengthens) the teeth.'

John Gerard *Herbal* (1597)

Did Tudor homes have kitchens?

DETECTIVE WORK

Find a book of Tudor recipes (see page 31). Do you recognise any of the ingredients used?

Early Tudor houses were made up of one big room, or hall. Everyone lived, slept and ate in this room. Food was cooked over the open fire. When houses were divided into storeys, with smaller rooms, there was space for a separate kitchen.

This painting shows many types of Tudor food.

Everything was cooked on the kitchen fire, which was never allowed to go out. At night the hot embers of the fire were covered with a type of lid called a 'curfew'. Then they were poked back into life the next morning. In large kitchens, there were spits for turning meat – sometimes dogs had the job of turning the machinery. The dog was trapped on a tread-wheel and had to keep walking until the meat was cooked.

Rich Tudors ate every kind of meat possible, from roast swan to wild boar. They also ate fine white 'manchet' bread made from wheat flour. Poor people could only afford brown bread, made from rye, barley and oats. Vegetables, which were cheaper than meat, made up most of their diet. But all Tudors were worried about eating fresh fruit – they thought it would upset their stomachs.

Most Tudors loved puddings and every kind of sweet food. They ate gingerbread decorated with real gold; 'marchpane', or marzipan; and jellies coloured purple by a plant called turnsole. Beer was very popular. Servants were allowed at least a gallon (4.5 litres) a day. Ladies drank the less bitter ale – and so did children!

An 'aumbrey' was a type of food cupboard. Air holes helped to keep food fresh.

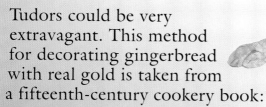

Tudors could be very extravagant. This method for decorating gingerbread with real gold is taken from a fifteenth-century cookery book:

'Take and cut your leaf of gold... into square pieces like dice, and with a... cony's [rabbit's] tail's end moisted a little, take the gold up by one corner, lay it on the place being first made moist, and with another tail of a cony, dry, press the gold down close.'

This wooden cake mould would leave the shape of a drummer on top of the cake.

How comfortable were Tudor homes?

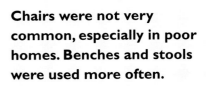

Ordinary people did not have much furniture. They just had a bed, a table, a chair, some stools, and perhaps a chest for storing linen or valuables. Most Tudor furniture was solid and plain, usually made of oak. Padded chairs were not very common, but there were cushions. Floors were made of tile or stone, but in the country, they were often just bare earth covered with straw or rushes.

Detective work

Try to visit a museum where old furniture is displayed. Also, look at any Tudor paintings showing the inside of houses. Make a list of the furniture and objects, and try to work out their use.

Chairs were not very common, especially in poor homes. Benches and stools were used more often.

Can you tell what sort of game the children are playing in the picture below?

Children playing games in the long gallery of a Tudor home.

Chimneys and windows made a great difference to comfort. Tudor homes became warmer and brighter. After dark, lighting was provided by candle or 'rushlight' (rushes dipped in fat). Beeswax candles smelled sweeter, but were expensive. Most people made their own smelly 'tallow' candles from animal fat.

In small houses, the 'hall' was still the space for sitting and talking, or playing games. Large houses had extra rooms, such as the long gallery. Here, rich families could take exercise in cold weather or listen to music being performed. Children could also play games that needed lots of space.

Carpets were too expensive to walk over. This carpet has been laid on a table for decoration.

Wallpaper was made in London after about 1520, but it was very expensive. However, rooms were sometimes made more colourful by travelling painters. Beams were often coloured red – perhaps as a protection against witches. Rich families could afford to panel walls, plaster ceilings and hang luxurious tapestries, but even the poor had painted cloths as decorations.

An Italian visitor was not impressed by the floors in English houses. Compare his description with Alessandro Magno's on page 5. Do you think things had improved by Magno's time?

The floors are strewed with clay and that covered with rushes which are now and then renewed, but not so as to disturb the foundation which sometimes remains for twenty years nursing a collection of spittle, vomits, excrement of dogs and human beings, spilt beer and fish bones and other filth which I need not mention.

Erasmus (1518)

What did the Tudors grow in their gardens?

A Tudor knot garden.

During Tudor times, explorers returned from all around the world with strange new plants. 'Love-apples' (tomatoes), potatoes, oranges and 'abricocks' (apricots) were introduced to Britain, as well as flowers such as laburnum, larkspur and Christmas roses. Tudor gardens were already filled with hollyhocks, wolfs bane, irises and marigolds. Flowers were not just for decoration – their petals were sometimes used in Tudor cookery and medicine.

With new plants, there was renewed interest in gardens. Owners of large houses loved to create gardens with magical patterns or pictures. Low hedges were filled with flowers and coloured stones. There were knot gardens which looked like tapestry designs, and mazes where hidden fountains might squirt you. Rich Tudors also liked to decorate their gardens with stone statues and topiary – hedges that were snipped and shaped into fantastic designs.

It must be a difficult task for gardeners to keep this Tudor garden in shape.

DETECTIVE WORK

Explore an old garden near your school (possibly as part of a visit to a Tudor house). Can you find some of the plants and flowers mentioned on pages 22 and 23?

At Hampton Court, King Henry VIII enclosed the flowerbeds with small green-and-white fences, and placed stone animals everywhere. In the gardens of other Tudor mansions, such as Ingatestone Hall, there were pavilions or summer houses. Guests would enjoy a 'banquet' here – the last course of their meals.

Poor people had gardens and fields around their cottages, where they could grow flax for making linen. Both large and small houses also grew food to eat: plums and gooseberries; 'worts' such as carrots and turnips for thick soups; herbs for flavouring and medicine. Caraway seeds were eaten with apples called 'pippins', which we still have today. Caraway was also a protection against witches, and might be given as a love potion.

Many new types of fruit appeared on Tudor tables, including apricots.

In William Shakespeare's play, *King Henry IV – Part II* (Act V Scene III), Justice Shallow proudly shows some friends around his orchard:

'Nay, you shall see mine orchard, where in an arbour (shady place), we will eat a last year's pippin (apple) of my own graffing (growing), with a dish of caraways (caraway seeds), and so forth...'

What were town houses like?

Even though London grew quickly during Tudor times, most Tudor towns would still seem very small to us. In 1603, London had a population of 200,000. Norwich was the second largest city, with only 11,000 people. Today it has a population of over 120,000.

Towns had many open spaces, but also great overcrowding, and there were many five-storey buildings. Because of the tall houses and 'jetties', town streets were dark and dirty. People were meant to put out a lantern at night and clean up their own rubbish, but many did not. Rats were everywhere – and Tudor doctors did not realize that they caused a terrible disease called the plague.

DETECTIVE WORK

Compare the map of London on this page with a modern map. Do any place names appear on both maps?

A Tudor picture map of 1563, showing the area around St Paul's Cathedral (top).

✿ How did the Tudor St Paul's differ from the cathedral we know today?

Rat catchers were kept busy. They shouted these words to advertise their services:

Rats or mice, ha' ye any rats, mice, polecats
*   or weasels*
Or ha' ye any old sows sick of the measels?
I can kill them, and I can kill moles,
*   and I can kill vermin that*
Creepeth up and creepeth down, and
*   peepeth into holes.*

British Museum

A town house was often used for trade. The shutters on ground-floor windows could be lowered down to make a shop counter. Apprentices (young boys learning a trade) and hired workers lived with the family, sleeping in the attic, and sharing meals. But the shop or workshop took up valuable living space. Gardens or yards were added to allow room for kitchens or storage buildings.

Risk of fire meant that it was safer to build the kitchen in brick with a stone floor. This separated it from the other rooms. Town authorities also tried to make people tile instead of thatch their roofs. This made it more difficult for flames to leap from house to house. But everyone still had to keep a fire bucket ready, and a hook to pull down any burning thatch.

Shops were made out of the front rooms of houses. The spectacle maker is doing a good trade!

Who lived at Ingatestone Hall?

*I*ngatestone Hall is a Tudor house in Essex, England. It was the home of Sir William Petre. He was an important man in the Tudor government who served four Tudor monarchs – without losing his head! His grand house was begun in 1540, and the Petre family live there still.

Life at Ingatestone was like living in a large village. This was because almost every job was done by someone on the estate – from the warrener (rabbit keeper) to the gardener. The older servants earnt £2 a year. They were also supplied with their summer and winter 'liveries' (uniforms) and their food and lodging.

Sir William Petre.

You had to be a rich person, like Sir William, to invite Queen Elizabeth I to stay, because she brought hundreds of followers with her. This is a small part of the list of supplies needed to look after the queen and other guests for four days. The full list was 20 times as long:

1 dozen wax lights, weight 3 lb (1.4 kg)
6 cygnets
27 geese
French wine, 10 gallons (45.5 litres)
693 eggs
44 dishes of butter
7 gallons (32 litres) of cream
200 oranges

Ingatestone Hall

Like many Tudor houses, Ingatestone was built around a courtyard, and it was up to date with its piped water system. There were special rooms for everything: a salt-house for keeping salt dry, a still-room for preparing herbs, and a 'buttery' – for beer, not butter! (It is named after an old word, 'butt', which means 'bottle'.) The dairy and the bakery were the most important work rooms. The household might eat 76 kg of cheese in one week. And in a year, the bakers might bake 20,000 loaves of bread!

Games were played in the long gallery at Ingatestone Hall.

🐾 Why was salt so important in Tudor times?

Ingatestone was a house of secrets, too. For a time it held a mysterious royal prisoner – Lady Catherine Grey.

Detective work

Using library books and the Internet, find out what happened to Lady Catherine Grey's more famous sister – Lady Jane Grey.

Ingatestone Hall stood beside a pond that was well stocked with fish. There was always fresh fish for the Petre table.

Your project

*I*f you have been following the detective work at the end of each section, you should have found plenty of clues. These clues will help you to produce your own project about a Tudor home.

First you will need to choose a topic that interests you. You could use one of the questions below as a starting point.

> **Topic questions**
> - What two important changes to houses might you have noticed, had you lived in Tudor times?
> - Compared to today, what rooms might be missing in an ordinary Tudor house?
> - How were different Tudor homes built?
> - What furniture would you expect to find in a Tudor house?

Half-timbered Tudor cottages.

When you have gathered all your information, present it in an interesting way. You might like to use one of the ideas below.

Project presentation
- Paint a large-scale, 'cut-away' Tudor house, as a wall display. Show the rooms, with furniture, objects and figures.
- Make a model of a timbered house, or shop. Use two different-sized shoe boxes, stuck bottom to bottom, to make the overhanging 'jetty'.
- Pretend you live in Tudor times. Write an invitation to a cousin, telling them all about your house.
- Imagine you are writing a play. Invent a scene where Elizabeth I attends a banquet.

A lively Tudor party in a banqueting hall.

Sherlock has produced a project about his Tudor ancestors. He has found out that some dogs were killed in 'bear-baiting' and others were made to turn kitchen spits. He thinks he would have enjoyed hunting, but on the whole he is not keen to be a Tudor dog!

Glossary

adze A tool for smoothing wood.

apprentices Children learning a trade.

aumbrey A food cupboard with air holes.

bedstead The Tudor word for the whole bed.

box bed A bed built into a wall.

close stool A small toilet, like a box.

curfew A way of making a fire safe at night.

cygnet A young swan.

gong farmer The person who cleared the lavatory pit.

inglenook An open area around a fire.

jakes The Tudor word for toilet.

jetty Where a storey on a building juts out further than the one beneath.

lath and plaster Flat strips of wood covered with plaster.

lattice window A window with diamond-shaped panes.

manchet The best quality white bread.

marchpane Marzipan.

pavilion A garden room for eating a dessert course.

pomander A holder for sweet-smelling herbs.

rushlight A wall light made from a rush dipped in tallow.

saw pit A pit where trees can be sawed.

tester A bed with a roof; a four-poster.

truckle A movable bed.

wattle and daub A mixture of sticks and clay used to fill between the beams in a wall.

Answers

page 5
❧ The smallest homes were not made of very good materials, just clay, wattle and daub, and straw-thatch, with no proper foundations or floors. They fell down and rotted over the years.

page 6
❧ This could have been to make more room or to shelter the lower floors from bad weather.

page 9
❧ It was easier because a wall was already here to support the new brickwork. In the middle of the house it would have needed a free-standing chimney stack. Moving the fire to one end also gave more space inside the house.

page 10
❧ The windows are highly decorative. Rich families sometimes included their 'coat of arms' in the design, as in this picture. This helped them show other people how important they were.

page 11
❧ If you look carefully, Bess has put her proper initials (E.S.) into the stonework on the very top of the house.

page 13
❧ The upholsterers were cheating people by pretending that their pillows or beds were full of expensive feathers, when they had added thistledown – which was free.

page 14
It is a toilet, specially padded for a royal bottom!

page 20
They are playing nine pins, the origin of our skittles and ten-pin bowling.

page 24
Our St Paul's Cathedral was built by Sir Christopher Wren, after the one shown here burnt down in the Great Fire of London in 1666. The new St Paul's has a round dome instead of a square tower.

page 27
Salt was very important for flavouring, but also for preserving food. There were no fridges in Tudor times to keep food fresh.

Books to read

Food and Cooking in 16th Century Britain
by Peter Brears (English Heritage, 1985)

Heritage: The Tudors in Britain
by Robert Hull (Hodder Wayland 2000)

My Tudor Home
by Karen Bryant-Mole (Watts Publishing, 2001)

Stories of Tudor Times
(Master Will's New Theatre)
by Alan Childs (Anglia Young Books, 1995)

The Tudors Reconstructed
by Liz Gogerly (Hodder Wayland, 2003)

Under the Rose
(A Tudor spy story set at Ingatestone Hall)
by Alan Childs (Anglia Young Books, 1991)

Who? What? When?: Tudors
by Bob Fowke (Hodder Children's Books, 2003)

Places to visit

Museum of Garden History
Lambeth Palace Rd, London SE1 7LB

Ingatestone Hall
Ingatestone, Essex, CM4 9NR
http://www.aboutbritain.com/IngatestoneHall.htm

Index

Numbers in **bold** refer to pictures and captions